Editorial review for Ascension by Amy Welborn

Ascension
PO Box 1990
West Chester, PA 19380
1-800-376-0520

ISBN 978-1-950784-48-6

Printed in the United States of America

ASCENSION
Kids

West Chester, PA

A Very Noisy Stable

by Jan Godfrey and Paula Doherty

"What a very noisy town!" thought Donkey, twitching his long ears,
trotting into Bethlehem, clip-clop, clip-clop,
with Mary and Joseph on that long-ago starry night.

"What a very noisy town!" thought Mary and Joseph,
looking for a place to rest on that long-ago starry night.
Rat-a-tat-tat!
"No room! No room!" shouted the innkeepers,
and they SHUT their doors – BANG!

At last Joseph found room in a rough and dirty stable.
Mary's baby would soon be born, and tonight she could rest
in the straw and the darkness, away from the noisy streets.

Donkey stood nearby, tired from his journey.
A very tiny spider sat in a cobwebby corner,
silently spinning a silky thread, all in a very quiet stable.

Donkey waited patiently under the stars.
He felt strangely excited, twitching his long ears,
as if something special was about to happen –
but what could it be?

Donkey kicked his hooves and lifted his head
and BRAYED very loudly.
"Hee-HAW!" brayed Donkey.
"Hee-HAW!!"

Donkey brayed so loudly that he woke up all the little mice in the stable.

"Eeek! Eeek!" squeaked the scampering mice.
They rustled the straw as they chased each other
in and out and round about all over the stable.

Nearby, some humpy, grumpy camels snored and snoozed.
"Hrrumphh!" snorted the camels,
spitting and grumbling at all the noise.

"Hee-HAW!" brayed Donkey.
"Eeek! Eeek!" squeaked the scampering mice.

Goat was tethered nearby and jumped about,
joining in all the commotion.
"Mehhh!" bleated Goat.

"Hee-HAW!" brayed Donkey.
"Eeek! Eeek!" squeaked the scampering mice.
"Hrrumphh!" snorted the humpy, grumpy camels.

Cow and Ox stood together in the stable, lumbering and heavy.

"Moo...ooo," bellowed Cow.

"What a to-DOO," boomed Ox.

"Hee-HAW!" brayed Donkey.

"Eeek! Eeek!" squeaked the scampering mice.
"Hrrumphh!" snorted the humpy, grumpy camels.
"Mehhh!" bleated Goat.

Owl flew over the stable, flapping her wings.

"Too-whit, too-whooo," hooted Owl.

"Hee-HAW!" brayed Donkey.

"Eeek! Eeek!" squeaked the scampering mice.

"Hrrumphh!" snorted the humpy, grumpy camels.

"Mehhh!" bleated Goat.

"Moo...ooo," bellowed Cow.

"What a to-DOO," boomed Ox.

A thin, hungry dog chased a skinny, scrawny cat.

"Woof! Woof!" howled hungry Dog.

"Meeow!" yowled skinny, scrawny Cat.

"Hee-HAW!" brayed Donkey.

"Eeek! Eeek!" squeaked the scampering mice.

"Hrrumphh!" snorted the humpy, grumpy camels.

"Mehhh!" bleated Goat.
"Moo...ooo," bellowed Cow.
"What a to-DOO," boomed Ox.
"Too-whit, too-whooo," hooted Owl.
It was PANDEMONIUM!
It was a HULLABALOO!
It was ... A VERY NOISY STABLE!!!

And then, suddenly, there was a great, deep silence
over all the whole wide world.
It was broken only by ... another noise, another sound,
the sound of a baby's happy cry.
"Aaah! Aaah!"

And angels shining with heavenly light
sang heavenly songs in the starry night:
"Glory to God," sang the angels,
"and peace to all on earth!
God's own Son has been born tonight!
He is lying in a manger in Bethlehem."

Donkey could hardly believe his long, twitching ears!
Had he really carried God's own Son
all the way to Bethlehem?

He nudged his way into the stable,
and there was the newborn baby Jesus asleep in the manger,
watched over by his blessed Mother and St. Joseph.
The animals were quiet now, and the tiny spider still sat silently spinning...

Then under the twinkling stars, sheep and shepherds ran to the stable.

"Baa! BAA!" bleated the sheep.

"Hee-HAW!" brayed Donkey.

"Eeek! Eeek!" squeaked the scampering mice.

"Hrrumphh!" snorted the humpy, grumpy camels.

"Mehhh!" bleated Goat.

"Moo...ooo," bellowed Cow.

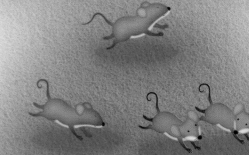

"What a to-DOO," boomed Ox.
"Too-whit, too-whooo," hooted Owl.
"Woof! Woof!" howled hungry Dog.
"Meeow!" yowled skinny, scrawny Cat.
All of them praised God in a very noisy stable
on that first Christmas night,
the night that Jesus Christ, God's Son, was born.